LOVE LETTERS
OF
GREAT MEN

Vol. 2

Love Poems

Published by SoHo Books
ISBN 978-1440495908
Printed in the USA

LOVE LETTERS OF GREAT MEN

Longing
by Matthew Arnold
(1822-1888)

Come to me in my dreams, and then

By day I shall be well again.

For then the night will more than pay

The hopeless longing of the day.

Come, as thou cam'st a thousand times,

A messenger from radiant climes,

And smile on thy new world, and be

As kind to others as to me.

Or, as thou never cam'st in sooth,

Come now, and let me dream it truth.

And part my hair, and kiss my brow,

And say My love! why sufferest thou?

Come to me in my dreams, and then

By day I shall be well again.

For then the night will more than pay

The hopeless longing of the day.

Love's Trinity
by Alfred Austin

Soul, heart, and body, we thus singly name,

Are not in love divisible and distinct,

But each with each inseparably link'd.

One is not honour, and the other shame,

But burn as closely fused as fuel, heat, and flame.

They do not love who give the body and keep

The heart ungiven; nor they who yield the soul,

And guard the body. Love doth give the whole;

Its range being high as heaven, as ocean deep,

Wide as the realms of air or planet's curving sweep

LOVE LETTERS OF GREAT MEN

My Suburban Girl
by Samuel Alfred Beadle

I know a sweet suburban girl,

She's witty, bright and brief;

With dimples in her cheeks; and pearl

In rubies set, for teeth.

Beneath her glossy raven hair

There beams the hazel eye,

Bright as the star of evening there

Where the yellow sunbeams die.

Her breath is like a flower blown,

In fragrance and perfume;

Her voice seems from the blissful throne

Where their harps the angels tune.

Her waist is just a trifle more

Than a cubit in its girth;

But when there my arms I throw,

I've all there is of earth.

And when she turns her dimpled cheek

Toward me for a kiss,

I lose expression - cannot speak -

And take all there is of bliss.

Because She Would Ask Me Why I Loved Her
by Christopher Brennan
(1870-1932)

If questioning would make us wise

No eyes would ever gaze in eyes;

If all our tale were told in speech

No mouths would wander each to each.

Were spirits free from mortal mesh

And love not bound in hearts of flesh

No aching breasts would yearn to meet

And find their ecstasy complete.

For who is there that lives and knows

The secret powers by which he grows?

Were knowledge all, what were our need

To thrill and faint and sweetly bleed?

Then seek not, sweet, the „If" and „Why"

I love you now until I die.

For I must love because I live

And life in me is what you give.

She Walks In Beauty
by Lord Byron

She walks in beauty, like the night

Of cloudless climes and starry skies;

And all that's best of dark and bright

Meet in her aspect and her eyes:

Thus mellow'd to that tender light

Which heaven to gaudy day denies.

One shade the more, one ray the less,

Had half impair'd the nameless grace

Which waves in every raven tress,

Or softly lightens o'er her face;

Where thoughts serenely sweet express

How pure, how dear their dwelling-place.

And on that cheek, and o'er that brow,

So soft, so calm, yet eloquent,

The smiles that win, the tints that glow,

But tell of days in goodness spent,

A mind at peace with all below,

A heart whose love is innocent!

A Red, Red Rose
by Robert Burns

O my luve's like a red, red rose.

That's newly sprung in June;

O my luve's like a melodie

That's sweetly play'd in tune.

As fair art thou, my bonnie lass,

So deep in luve am I;

And I will love thee still, my Dear,

Till a'the seas gang dry.

Till a' the seas gang dry, my Dear,

And the rocks melt wi' the sun:

I will luve thee still, my Dear,

While the sands o'life shall run.

And fare thee weel my only Luve!

And fare thee weel a while!

And I will come again, my Luve,

Tho' it were ten thousand mile!

First Love

by John Clare

I ne'er was struck before that hour

With love so sudden and so sweet.

Her face it bloomed like a sweet flower

And stole my heart away complete.

My face turned pale, a deadly pale.

My legs refused to walk away,

And when she looked what could I ail

My life and all seemed turned to clay.

And then my blood rushed to my face

And took my eyesight quite away.

The trees and bushes round the place

Seemed midnight at noonday.

I could not see a single thing,

Words from my eyes did start.

They spoke as chords do from the string,

And blood burnt round my heart.

Are flowers the winter's choice

Is love's bed always snow

She seemed to hear my silent voice

Not love appeals to know.

I never saw so sweet a face

As that I stood before.

My heart has left its dwelling place

And can return no more.

Song Of Secret Love
by John Clare

I hid my love when young while I

Couldn't bear the buzzing of a fly

I hid my love to my despite

Till I could not bear to look at light

I dare not gaze upon her face

But left her memory in each place

Where ere I saw a wild flower lie

I kissed and bade my love goodbye

I met her in the greenest dells

Where dew drops pearl the wood bluebells

The lost breeze kissed her bright blue eye

The bee kissed and went singing by

A sunbeam found a passage there

A gold chain round her neck so fair

As secret as the wild bee's song

She lay there all the summer long

I hid my love in field and town

Till e'en the breeze would knock me down

The bees seemed singing ballads l'er

The fly's buss turned a Lion's roar

And even silence found a tongue

To haunt me all the summer long

The riddle nature could not prove

Was nothing else but secret love

Love
by Samuel Taylor Coleridge

And in Life's noisiest hour,

There whispers still the ceaseless Love of Thee,

The heart's Self-solace and soliloquy.

You mould my Hopes, you fashion me within ;

And to the leading Love-throb in the Heart

Thro' all my Being, thro' my pulse's beat ;

You lie in all my many Thoughts, like Light,

Like the fair light of Dawn, or summer Eve

On rippling Stream, or cloud-reflecting Lake.

And looking to the Heaven, that bends above you,

How oft! I bless the Lot that made me love you.

Damelus' Song to Diaphenia
by Henry Constable
(1562-1613)

Diaphenia, like the daffadowndilly,

White as the sun, fair as the lily,

Heigh ho, how I do love thee!

I do love thee as my lambs

Are belovëd of their dams -

How blest were I if thou wouldst prove me!

Diaphenia, like the spreading roses,

That in thy sweets all sweets incloses,

Fair sweet, how I do love thee!

I do love thee as each flower

Loves the sun's life-giving power,

For, dead, thy breath to life might move me.

Diaphenia, like to all things blessed,

When all thy praises are expressëd,

Dear joy, how I do love thee!

As the birds do love the spring,

Or the bees their careful king, -

Then in requite, sweet virgin, love me!

To a Young Lady
by William Cowper

Sweet stream that winds through yonder glade,

Apt emblem of a virtuous maid

Silent and chaste she steals along,

Far from the world's gay busy throng:

With gentle yet prevailing force,

Intent upon her destined course;

Graceful and useful all she does,

Blessing and blest where'er she goes;

Pure-bosom'd as that watery glass,

And Heaven reflected in her face.

Farewell to Love
by Michael Drayton
(1563-1631)

Since there's not help, come let us kiss and part;

Nay, I am done, you get no more of me;

And I am glad, yea, glad with all my heart,

That thus so cleanly I myself can free;

Shake hands for ever, cancel all our vows,

And when we meet at any time again,

Be it not seen in either of our brows

That we, one jot of former love retain.

Now, at the last gasp of love's latest breath,

When his pulse failing, passion speechless lies,

When faith is kneeling by his bed of death,

And innocence is closing up his eyes,

Now, if thou woulds't, when all have given him over,

From death to life Thou might'st him yet recover.

Felix Holt, the Radical
George Eliot
(1819-1880)

Why, there are maidens of heroic touch

And yet they seem like things of gossamer

You'd pinch the life out of, as out of moths.

O, it is not fond tones and mouthingness,

'Tis not the arms akimbo and large strides,

That makes a woman's force. The tiniest birds,

With softest downy breasts, have passion in them,

And are brave with love.

Thomas Ford

There is a Lady Sweet and Kind

There is a lady sweet and kind,

Was never a face so pleased my mind;

I did but see her passing by,

And yet I'll love her till I die.

Her gesture, motion, and her smiles,

Her wit, her voice my heart beguiles,

Beguiles my heart, I know not why,

And yet I'll love her till I die.

Cupid is winged and he doth range,

Her country, so, my love doth change:

But change she earth, or change she sky,

Yet, I will love her till I die.

Beautiful Dreamer
by Stephen Foster

Beautiful dreamer, wake unto me,

Starlight and dewdrops are waiting for thee;

Sounds of the rude world heard in the day,

Lull'd by the moonlight have all pass'd a way!

Beautiful dreamer, queen of my song,

List while I woo thee with soft melody;

Gone are the cares of life's busy throng, --

Beautiful dreamer, awake unto me!

Beautiful dreamer, out on the sea

Mermaids are chaunting the wild lorelie;

Over the streamlet vapors are borne,

Waiting to fade at the bright coming morn.

Beautiful dreamer, beam on my heart,

E'en as the morn on the streamlet and sea;

Then will all clouds of sorrow depart, --

Beautiful dreamer, awake unto me!

To Earthward
by Robert Frost

Love at the lips was touch

As sweet as I could bear;

And once that seemed too much;

I lived on air

That crossed me from sweet things,

The flow of - was it musk

From hidden grapevine springs

Down hill at dusk?

I had the swirl and ache

From sprays of honeysuckle

That when they're gathered shake

Dew on the knuckle.

I craved strong sweets, but those

Seemed strong when I was young;

The petal of the rose

It was that stung.

Now no joy but lacks salt

That is not dashed with pain

And weariness and fault;

I crave the stain

Of tears, the aftermark

Of almost too much love,

The sweet of bitter bark

And burning clove.

When stiff and sore and scarred

I take away my hand

From leaning on it hard

In grass and sand,

The hurt is not enough:

I long for weight and strength

To feel the earth as rough

To all my length.

Reluctance
by Thomas Frost

Out through the fields and the woods

And over the walls I have wended;

I have climbed the hills of view

And looked at the world, and descended;

I have come by the highway home,

And lo, it is ended.

The leaves are all dead on the ground,

Save those that the oak is keeping

To ravel them one by one

And let them go scraping and creeping

Out over the crusted snow,

When others are sleeping.

And the dead leaves lie huddled and still,

No longer blown hither and thither;

The last lone aster is gone;

The flowers of the witch hazel wither;

The heart is still aching to seek,

But the feet question „Whither?"

Ah, when to the heart of man

Was it ever less than a treason

To go with the drift of things,

To yield with a grace to reason,

And bow and accept the end

Of a love or a season?

Wind and Window Flower
by Robert Frost

Lovers, forget your love,

And list to the love of these,

She a window flower,

And he a winter breeze.

When the frosty window veil

Was melted down at noon,

And the caged yellow bird

Hung over her in tune,

He marked her through the pane,

He could not help but mark,

And only passed her by

To come again at dark.

He was a winter wind,

Concerned with ice and snow,

Dead weeds and unmated birds,

And little of love could know.

But he sighed upon the sill,

He gave the sash a shake,

As witness all within

Who lay that night awake.

Perchance he half prevailed

To win her for the flight

From the firelit looking-glass

And warm stove-window light.

But the flower leaned aside

And thought of naught to say,

And morning found the breeze

A hundred miles away.

Love and a question
by Thomas Frost

A stranger came to the door at eve,

And he spoke the bridegroom fair.

He bore a green-white stick in his hand,

And, for all burden, care.

He asked with the eyes more than the lips

For a shelter for the night,

And he turned and looked at the road afar

Without a window light.

The bridegroom came forth into the porch

With, „Let us look at the sky,

And question what of the night to be,

Stranger, you and I."

The woodbine leaves littered the yard,

The woodbine berries were blue,

Autumn, yes, winter was in the wind;

„Stranger, I wish I knew."

Within, the bride in the dusk alone

Bent over the open fire,

Her face rose-red with the glowing coal

And the thought of the heart's desire.

The bridegroom looked at the weary road,

Yet saw but her within,

And wished her heart in a case of gold

And pinned with a silver pin.

The bridegroom thought it little to give

A dole of bread, a purse,

A heartfelt prayer for the poor of God,

Or for the rich a curse;

But whether or not a man was asked

To mar the love of two

by harboring woe in the bridal house,

The bridegroom wished he knew.

My Country Love
by Norman Rowland Gale

If you passed her in your city

You would call her badly dressed,

But the faded homespun covers

Such a heart in such a breast!

True, her rosy face is freckled

By the sun's abundant flame,

But she's mine with all her failings,

And I love her just the same.

If her hands are red they grapple

To my hands with splendid strength,

For she's mine, all mine's the beauty

Of her straight and lovely length!

True, her hose be think and homely

And her speech is homely, too;

But she's mine! her rarest charm is

She's for me, and not for you!

Night Thoughts
by Johann Wolfgang von Goethe

Stars, you are unfortunate, I pity you,

Beautiful as you are, shining in your glory,

Who guide seafaring men through stress and peril

And have no recompense from gods or mortals,

Love you do not, nor do you know what love is.

Hours that are aeons urgently conducting

Your figures in a dance through the vast heaven,

What journey have you ended in this moment,

Since lingering in the arms of my beloved

I lost all memory of you and midnight.

My Love's A Match
by Alfred P. Graves

My Love's a match in beauty

For every flower that blows,

Her little ear's a lilly,

Her velvet cheek a rose;

Her locks are gilly gowans

Hang golden to her knee.

If I were King of Ireland,

My Queen she'd surely be.

Her eyes are fond forget-me-nots,

And no such snow is seen

Upon the heaving hawthorn bush

As crests her bodice green.

The thrushes when she's talking

Sit listening on the tree.

If I were King of Ireland,

My Queen she'd surely be.

Upon Julia's Clothes
by Robert Herrick

Whenas in silks my Julia goes,

Then, then, methinks, how sweetly flows

The liquefaction of her clothes.

Next, when I cast mine eyes, and see

That brave vibration, each way free,

Oh, how that glittering taketh me!

Sweet Disorder
by Robert Herrick

A sweet disorder in the dress

Kindles in clothes a wantonness:

A lawn about the shoulders thrown

Into a fine distraction -

An erring lace, which here and there

Enthrals the crimson stomacher -

A cuff neglectful, and thereby

Ribbands to flow confusedly -

A winning wave, deserving note,

In the tempestuous petticoat -

A careless shoe-string, in whose tie

I see a wild civility -

Do more bewitch me than when art

Is too precise in every part.

To the Virgins, Make Much of Time
by Robert Herrick

Gather ye rosebuds while ye may,

Old time is still a-flying,

And this same flower that smiles today,

To-morrow will be dying.

The glorious lamp of heaven, the sun,

The higher he's a-getting,

The sooner will his race be run,

And nearer he's to setting.

That age is best which is the first,

When youth and blood are warmer;

But being spent, the worse and worst

Times still succeed the former.

Then be not coy, but use your time,

and while ye may, go marry;

For having lost just once your prime,

You may for ever tarry.

To Anthea
by Robert Herrick

Bid me to live, and I will live

Thy Protestant to be;

Or bid me love, and I will give

A loving heart to thee.

A heart as soft, a heart as kind,

A heart as sound and free

As in the whole world thou canst find,

That heart I'll give to thee.

Bid that heart stay, and it will stay

To honor thy decrees:

Or bid it languish quite away,

And't shall do so for thee.

Bid me to weep, and I will weep

While I have eyes to see:

And, having none, yet I will keep

A heart to weep for thee.

Bid me despair and I'll despair

Under that cypress-tree:

Or bid me die, and I will dare

E'en death to die for thee.

Thou art my life, my love, my heart,

The very eyes of me:

And hast command of every part

To live and die for thee.

Jenny Kissed Me
by **Leigh Hunt**

Jenny kissed me when we met,

Jumping from the chair she sat in;

Time, you thief, who love to get

Sweets into your list, put that in:

Say I'm weary, say I'm sad,

Say that health and wealth have missed me,

Say I'm growing old, but add,

Jenny kissed me.

Still to be Neat
by Benjamin Jonson

Still to be neat, still to be drest,

As you were going to a feast;

Still to be powder'd, still perfum'd:

Lady, it is to be presum'd,

Though art's hid causes are not found,

All is not sweet, all is not sound.

Give me a look, give me a face,

That make simplicity a grace;

Robes loosely flowing, hair as free:

Such sweet neglect more taketh me

Than all th'adulteries of art.

They strike mine eyes, but not my heart.

To Cecilia
by Benjamin Jonson

Drink to me, only with thine eyes

And I will pledge with mine;

Or leave a kiss but in the cup,

And I'll not look for wine.

The thirst that from the soul doth rise

Doth ask a drink divine:

But might I of Jove's nectar sup

I would not change for thine.

I sent thee late a rosy wreath,

Not so much honouring thee

As giving it a hope that there

It could not withered be

But thou thereon didst only breath

And sent'st it back to me:

Since, when it grows and smells, I swear,

Not of itself but thee.

When I Have Fears That I May Cease To Be
by John Keats

When I have fears that I may cease to be

Before my pen has glean'd my teeming brain,

Before high-piled books, in charactery,

Hold like rich garners the full ripen'd grain;

When I behold, upon the night's starr'd face,

Huge cloudy symbols of a high romance,

And think that I may never live to trace

Their shadows, with the magic hand of chance;

And when I feel, fair creature of an hour,

That I shall never look upon thee more,

Never have relish in the faery power

Of unreflecting love;--then on the shore

Of the wide world I stand alone, and think

Till love and fame to nothingness do sink.

Tell Me Not, Sweet
by Richard Lovelace

Tell me not, Sweet, I am unkind

For, from the nunnery

Of thy chaste breast, and quiet mind,

To war and arms I fly.

True, a new mistress now I chase,

The first foe in the field;

And with a stronger faith- embrace

A sword, a horse, a shield.

Yet this unconstancy is such

As you too shall adore;

For, I could not love thee, Dear, so much,

Loved I not honour more.

Naked
by Pablo Neruda

Naked, you are simple as a hand,

smooth, earthy, small...transparent, round.

You have moon lines and apple paths;

Naked, you are slender as the wheat.

Naked, Cuban blue midnight is your color,

Naked, I trace the stars and vines in your hair;

Naked, you are spacious and yellow

As a summer's wholeness in a golden church.

Naked, you are tiny as your fingernail;

Subtle and curved in the rose-colored dawn

And you withdraw to the underground world

As if down a long tunnel of clothing and of chores:

your clear light dims, gets dressed, drops its leaves,

And becomes a naked hand again.

A Dream within a Dream
by Edgar Allen Poe

Take this kiss upon the brow!

And, in parting from you now,

Thus much let me avow-

You are not wrong, who deem

That my days have been a dream;

Yet, if Hope has flown away

In a night, or in a day,

In a vision, or in none,

Is it, therefore, the less gone?

All that we see or seem

Is but a dream within a dream.

I stand amid the roar

Of a surf-tormented shore,

And I hold within my hand

Grains of golden sand-

How few! yet how they creep

Through my fingers to the deep,

While I weep- while I weep!

O God! can I not grasp

Them with a tighter clasp?

O God! can I not save

One from the pitiless wave?

Is all that we see or seem

But a dream within a dream?

Sonnet 44

by William Shakespeare

If the dull substance of my flesh were thought,

Injurious distance should not stop my way.

For then, despite of space, I would be brought

From limits far remote where thou dost stay.

No matter then although my foot did stand

Upon the farthest earth removed from thee.

For nimble thought can jump both sea and land

As soon as think the place where he would be.

But, ah, thought kills me, that I am not thought,

To leap large length of miles when thou art gone,

But that, so much of earth and water wrought,

I must attend times leisure with my moan,

Receiving naught by elements so slow

But heavy tears, badges of either's woe.

The Lost Thrill
by James Whitcomb Riley

I grow so weary, someway, of all things

That love and loving have vouchsafed to me,

Since now all dreamed-of sweets of ecstasy

Am I possessed of: The caress that clings -

The lips that mix with mine with murmurings

No language may interpret, and the free,

Unfettered brood of kisses, hungrily

Feasting in swarms on honeyed blossomings

Of passion's fullest flower - For yet I miss

The essence that alone makes love divine -

The subtle flavoring no tang of this

Weak wine of melody may here define:

A something found and lost in the first kiss

A lover ever poured through lips of mine.

Again and Again
by Rainer Maria Rilke

Again and again, however we know the landscape of love

and the little churchyard there, with its sorrowing names,

and the frighteningly silent abyss into which the others

fall: again and again the two of us walk out together

under the ancient trees, lie down again and again

among the flowers, face to face with the sky.

Beauty and Love
Andrew Young

Beauty and love are all my dream;

They change not with the changing day;

Love stays forever like a stream

That flows but never flows away;

And beauty is the bright sun-bow

That blossoms on the spray that showers

Where the loud water falls below,

Making a wind among the flowers.

Go, Lovely Rose
Edmund Waller

Tell her that wastes her time and me,

That now she knows,

When I resemble her to thee,

How sweet and fair she seems to be.

Tell her that ,s young,

And shuns to have her graces spied,

That hadst thou sprung

In deserts where no men abide,

Thou must have uncommended died.

Small is the worth

Of beauty from the light retired:

Bid her come forth,

Suffer herself to be desired,

And not blush so to be admired.

Then die - that she

The common fate of all things rare

May read in thee;

How small a part of time they share

That are so wondrous sweet and fair!

Love not me
by John Wilbye

Love not me for comely grace,

For my pleasing eye or face,

Nor for any outward part:

No, nor for a constant heart!

For these may fail or turn to ill:

Should thou and I sever.

Keep, therefore, a true woman's eye,

And love me still, but know not why!

So hast thou the same reason still

To dote upon me ever.

To Amarantha
by Richard Lovelace

Amarantha sweet and fair,

Ah, braid no more that shining hair!

As my curious hand or eye

Hovering round thee, let it fly!

Let it fly as unconfined

As its calm ravisher the wind,

Who hath left his darling, th' East,

To wanton o'er that spicy nest.

Every tress must be confest,

But neatly tangled at the best;

Like a clew of golden thread

Most excellently ravell d.

Do not then wind up that light

In ribbands, and o'er cloud in night,

Like the Sun's early ray;

But shake your head, and scatter day!

She comes not

by Herbert Trench

She comes not when Noon is on the roses -

Too bright is Day.

She comes not to the Soul till it reposes

From work and play.

But when Night is on the hills,

and the great Voices Roll in from Sea,

By starlight and candle-light and dreamlight

She comes to me.

ALSO AVAILABLE:

Love Letter of Great Men

Vol. 1

49773409R00057

Made in the USA
Columbia, SC
26 January 2019